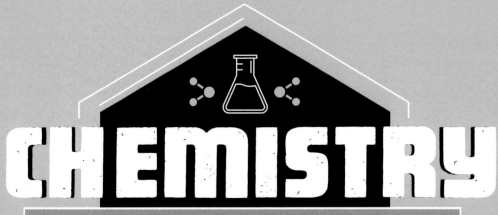

CHEMISTRY

PROJECTS TO BUILD ON

4D An Augmented Reading Experience

BY MARNE VENTURA

CONSULTANT: TOM HONZ

Teacher Librarian/Media Specialist
Centennial High School
Ankeny, Iowa

CAPSTONE PRESS
a capstone imprint

Dabble Lab is published by Capstone Press,
1710 Roe Crest Drive, North Mankato, Minnesota 56003
www.mycapstone.com

Library of Congress Cataloging-in-Publication Data
ISBN 978-1-5435-2848-0 (library binding)
ISBN 978-1-5435-2852-7 (paperback)
ISBN 978-1-5435-2856-5 (eBook PDF)

Editorial Credits:
Mari Bolte, editor; Heidi Thompson, designer; Morgan Walters, media researcher;
Laura Manthe, production specialist

Photo Credits:
All images by Capstone Studio, Karon Dubke
Shutterstock: 4 Girls 1 Boy, (grid) design element throughout, David Tadevosian, 5, VectorPot (gears)
design element throughout

Printed in the United States of America.
PA49

TABLE OF CONTENTS

BUBBLE AND POP!

Hiss, pop, whoosh! Chemists are always studying matter and how it changes. Gas bubbles, growing things, and frozen crystals are all results of chemical reactions.

Learn the science behind these fizzy mysteries by re-creating them yourself. You may be starting out with balloons and bubbles, but keep on practicing. Someday your chemistry skills could get a good reaction!

① Ask an adult to download the app.  Capstone 4D Education

② Scan any page with the star.

③ Enjoy your cool stuff!

— OR —

Use this password at capstone4D.com

nextlevel.chemistry

★ AIRHEAD

A chemical reaction occurs when two substances are mixed together to form something new. Become a chemist by mixing up your own reaction.

MAGIC BALLOON

What happens when you combine baking soda and vinegar? The results might surprise you!

YOU'LL NEED

> small funnel

> 2 tablespoons (30 grams) baking soda

> balloon

> plastic water bottle, cap removed

> 2 tablespoons (30 milliliters) white vinegar

> blue food coloring

STEPS

1. Use the funnel to pour the baking soda into the balloon.

2. Set the funnel over the bottle. Pour the vinegar into the bottle, and then remove the funnel.

FACT Everything is made of tiny particles, or pieces, called atoms. Multiple atoms connect to make molecules. A molecule is the smallest unit of a substance, such as water or gas. For example, water is made of two hydrogen atoms and one oxygen atom—H_2O. A single H_2O combination is a molecule.

3 Add a few drops of food coloring.

4 Stretch the mouth of the balloon over the opening of the water bottle. Be careful not to let the baking soda fall into the bottle.

5 When the balloon is secure, tip the bottle. The vinegar and baking soda should mix.

6 Set the bottle upright, and watch the balloon inflate.

FACT When baking soda (a base) and vinegar (an acid) are mixed together, they combine to form something new. This reaction makes a gas called carbon dioxide. The molecules in the gas rise and spread out. Gas molecules pushing against the inside of the balloon cause it to expand.

FIZZ-POWERED BOAT

The Magic Balloon collected all the energy created by the vinegar and baking soda. You can put that energy to work for you with this fizz-powered boat.

YOU'LL NEED

> utility knife

> plastic bottle with lid

> scissors

> drinking straw

> hot glue and hot glue gun

> ½ cup (120 mL) white vinegar

> 2 tablespoons (30 g) baking soda

> large tub of water

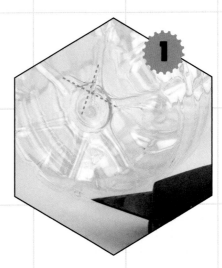

STEPS

1 Ask an adult to cut a small X in the bottom of the bottle. It should be about 1 inch (2.5 centimeters) from the bottle's edge.

FACT Expanding carbon dioxide gas pushes out of the bottle. The straw helps the gas escape. The escaping gas pushes the boat forward on the water's surface.

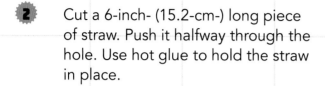

2. Cut a 6-inch- (15.2-cm-) long piece of straw. Push it halfway through the hole. Use hot glue to hold the straw in place.

3. Pour the vinegar into the bottle.

4. Add the baking soda. Screw on the bottle cap.

5. Tip the bottle to mix the vinegar and baking soda.

6. Place the bottle in the tub of water, and then watch your boat move!

 FACT The scientific name for baking soda is sodium bicarbonate. Baking soda is called a base. When you mix baking soda and an acidic ingredient like vinegar, it creates carbon dioxide gas. In the kitchen, you mix baking soda with acidic ingredients like lemon juice, brown sugar, dairy products, or fruit. Those combinations make fluffy cakes and soft cookies.

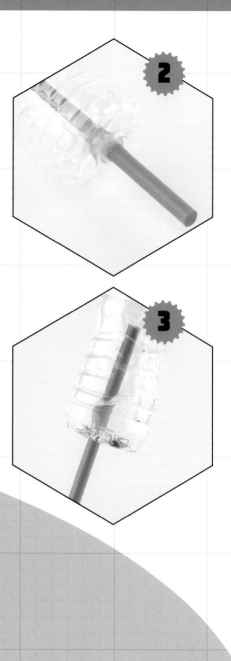

The Magic Balloon inflated as it collected gas. The straw in the Fizz-Powered Boat let the gas escape. But what happens when there is nowhere for carbon dioxide gas to go as it expands? Try this activity to find out.

YOU'LL NEED

> scissors

> paper towel

> 1 ½ tablespoons (23 g) baking soda

> ½ cup (120 mL) white vinegar

> ¼ cup (60 mL) warm water

> food coloring

> sandwich-sized zip-top bag

STEPS

1 Find an outdoor space where it's OK to spill liquid.

2 Cut a paper towel into a 5-inch (13-cm) square.

3 Pour the baking soda into the center of the paper towel.

3

4 Fold the towel into a tight packet, with the soda in the center.

5 Pour the vinegar, water, and food coloring into the sandwich bag.

6 Place the paper towel inside the bag, but don't let it touch the vinegar and water.

7 Close the bag firmly.

8 Shake the bag. Set it quickly on the ground, and step away.

 FACT In this experiment, the expanding gas has nowhere to go. It keeps expanding until the building pressure causes the bag to explode. The paper towel delayed the vinegar from reaching the baking powder, giving you enough time to safely set the bag on the ground.

IT'S ALIVE

In the last section, you mixed an acid and a base to make carbon dioxide. That's not the only way you can do it, though! Yeast makes carbon dioxide too. Like baking soda, yeast is a leavener. It's what helps bread rise up and become fluffy. Learn more about how yeast grows.

Yeast's favorite food is sugar. It eats the sugar and makes carbon dioxide. This is called anaerobic fermentation. The carbon dioxide is trapped in the dough, leaving air pockets behind. Find out what kind of sugar yeast likes best.

 YOU'LL NEED

> permanent marker

> 5 plastic water bottles, caps removed

> 5 packets of yeast

> measuring cup/spoons

> 4 tablespoons (60 g) white sugar

> 2 tablespoons (30 g) brown sugar

> 2 tablespoons (30 mL) honey

> water

> 5 balloons

STEPS

 1. Use a permanent marker to label your bottles. The labels should say:

a. Bottle 1: No Sugar

b. Bottle 2: White Sugar, Cold Water

c. Bottle 3: White Sugar

d. Bottle 4: Brown Sugar

e. Bottle 5: Honey

2 Pour a packet of yeast into each water bottle. Set the No Sugar bottle aside.

3 Add 2 tablespoons of white sugar to both the second and third bottles.

4 In the fourth bottle, add the brown sugar.

5 In the fifth bottle, add the honey.

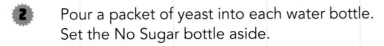

 FACT The ideal water temperature for yeast is 110 to 115 degrees Fahrenheit (43 to 46 degrees Celsius). Use a thermometer for the most accurate temperature for your yeast.

6 Measure and pour ¼ cup (60 mL) of cold tap water into the second bottle. Set aside.

7 Have an adult help you gently heat 2 cups (480 mL) of water. The water should be just a little warmer than your body temperature. Touch the outside of the measuring cup. If it's not too hot to the touch, carefully stick your finger in the water. If the water is too hot for your finger, it's too hot for the yeast.

8 Pour ¼ cup of warm water into each remaining bottle. Immediately fit a balloon over the mouth of each bottle.

White Sugar
Cold Water

TRY THIS Want to test your yeast beforehand? Dissolve 1 teaspoon (5 g) of white sugar in ½ cup (120 mL) warm water. Stir in a packet of yeast. If your yeast is good, it will start to rise after several minutes. After 10 minutes, it will have doubled in size. If the yeast did not rise, throw it away and buy new yeast.

9 Observe your bottles and balloons after 30 minutes, 1 hour, 2 hours, 4 hours, and overnight. Which balloons filled up the fastest? Which ones were the largest? Which had the slowest reactions?

 FACT Yeast is a living single-celled microorganism that feeds off sugars. It takes 20 billion yeast cells to get one gram of baking yeast. The yeast you can buy in packets is alive but inactive. Moisture helps activate it.

FABULOUS FOAM

Yeast is a catalyst. A catalyst is a substance that gets chemical reactions started and speeds them up. But it doesn't take part in the reaction itself or change the materials used in the chemical reaction. Watch yeast in action as it helps make a foamy mess!

YOU'LL NEED

> 5 packets of yeast

> 5 disposable cups

> measuring cups

> 2 ½ cups (600 mL) of warm water

> spoon

> dish soap

> 5 empty plastic water bottles

> food coloring in 5 different colors

> safety goggles and gloves

> funnel

> 40-volume hydrogen peroxide

> 5 disposable baking pans

STEPS

1   Pour a packet of yeast into a disposable cup. Repeat with the remaining yeast packets and cups.

2   Pour ¼ cup (60 mL) of warm water into each cup. Stir to help the yeast dissolve. Set aside.

TIP Drugstores sell 3 percent hydrogen peroxide. It's not strong enough for this activity. You can find 40-volume hydrogen peroxide at stores that sell hair care products.

3 Squirt about a tablespoon (15 mL) of dish soap into each bottle. Add a different color of food coloring to each.

4 Put on your safety goggles and gloves. With an adult's help, measure and pour peroxide into the bottles in the following amounts:

    a.   Bottle 1: no peroxide

    b.   Bottle 2: 1 tablespoon

    c.   Bottle 3: 2 tablespoons (30 mL)

    d.   Bottle 4: 3 tablespoons (45 mL)

    e.   Bottle 5: 4 tablespoons (60 mL)

5 Swirl each bottle to gently mix the contents.

6 Set each bottle in its own baking pan.

TIP Make sure that you're doing this experiment in an area that can get wet and won't be damaged by hydrogen peroxide or food coloring.

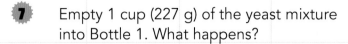

7 Empty 1 cup (227 g) of the yeast mixture into Bottle 1. What happens?

8 Repeat with the remaining bottles and yeast. Record what happens with each bottle. Which bottle gets the biggest reaction? How are the reactions different?

9 Go back and add peroxide to Bottle 1. What happens?

WHAT HAPPENED?

The 40-volume contains 16 percent hydrogen peroxide. It releases 40 times its volume in oxygen. The oxygen is trapped in the dish soap, creating foam. Without the peroxide, the yeast can't act as a catalyst. The reaction will also be limited to how much peroxide has been added. The more peroxide you add, the more foam will be produced. However, if you add too much peroxide, the enzyme in the yeast won't be able to keep up. Add more yeast and the reaction will continue.

YUMMY YEAST

You've learned that yeast produces carbon dioxide as it eats sugar, and that it acts as a catalyst. How do carbon dioxide and catalysts work in our everyday lives? Make your own sourdough starter to find out. Sourdough starter is a mix of flour and liquid. The wild yeast in the flour lives and grows. Who needs a pet rock when you can have a pet that's really alive?

YOU'LL NEED

FOR THE STARTER

> all-purpose flour

> measuring spoons

> unsweetened pineapple juice

> mason jar with a lid

> ruler

> dry erase marker

YOU'LL NEED

FOR THE BREAD

> 1 cup (227 g) sourdough starter

> 1 ½ cups (360 mL) warm water

> 1 packet yeast

> 2 teaspoons (10 g) salt

> 5 cups (1135 g) flour

> olive oil

> baking sheet

> clean towel

> spray bottle

> plain white sandwich bread

STEPS

1 Start by smelling the flour. Then taste it. Record your observations.

2 Measure and pour 2 tablespoons (30 g) of flour and 2 tablespoons (30 mL) of pineapple juice into the mason jar. Do not stir. Record what your mixture looks and smells like.

3 Use a ruler and dry erase marker to record the height of the mixture. Cover the jar with the lid. Let it sit at room temperature for 24 hours.

FACT Flour is what's known as a complex carbohydrate. When you eat it dry, you won't taste much. Your body can't tell the different molecules apart. But when the flour gets wet, enzymes in flour and wild yeast work as catalysts. They break the flour's starches apart into simpler sugar molecules. Then the yeast eats the sugar.

4 On the second day, repeat steps 2 and 3. This time, stir the mixture. Does the mixture look or smell any different? Erase the old mark and measure the new height.

5 On the third day, repeat steps 2–4.

6 On the fourth day, give your starter a stir. Measure out ¼ cup (60 mL) and discard. Stir in ¼ cup (57 g) each of flour and filtered water. Record the starter's smell and height before and after feeding the starter.

 FACT If you don't discard part of your starter, it will continue to grow. You will quickly run out of space in your jar!

7 Repeat step 6 daily for the next 10 days.

8 Continue feeding without discarding until you have 1 cup of starter.

9 To turn your starter into bread, mix the sourdough starter, water, yeast, salt, and flour together in a large bowl. Knead until it's smooth.

10 Pour a little olive oil into another large bowl. Rub the oil around the bowl to coat all the sides. Place the dough in the bowl.

11 Cover the bowl and let the dough rise until doubled in size, about 90 minutes.

12 Divide the dough into two balls. Gently shape the balls into oval-shaped loaves. Place the loaves on a lightly greased baking sheet. Cover with a clean towel and let rise for about 1 hour.

13 With an adult's help, preheat the oven to 425 degrees Fahrenheit (220 degrees Celsius).

14 Fill the spray bottle with warm water. Gently mist both loaves.

TIP Not ready to bake yet? Move your starter to the refrigerator. Feed it every few days during week 3, and then once a week after that. When you're ready to use it, take it out of the refrigerator. Discard all but ½ cup (125 mL), and add ½ cup each of flour and water. Let rest overnight at room temperature. Repeat until the starter is bubbly, at least doubled in size, and is the right quantity for your recipe. It will smell sour but fresh.

15 Ask an adult to use a knife to make two deep slashes in each loaf. This will help steam escape as the bread bakes.

16 Bake the bread for 25–30 minutes. Have an adult remove the bread from the oven. Let it cool completely on a cooling rack.

17 Have an adult cut the loaves into slices. Compare your sourdough bread to the sandwich bread. Do they taste different? Look at the holes inside the bread. Are they the same size? Which is larger? Why do you think that is?

★ GROW IT

When you think "chemistry," you probably don't think "plants." But photosynthesis, the process that plants use to breathe and make food, is a chemical reaction! It may not be fast or flashy, but in the end you'll have something you can show off and share.

Plants use the energy from light to turn carbon dioxide and water into food. The food helps the plants grow. What happens if you limit the amount of light your plant receives?

 **YOU'LL NEED**

> 3 small pots   > chive seeds

> potting soil   > watering can

STEPS

1 Fill each pot 2/3 of the way with potting soil.

2 Use your finger to poke a hole in the middle of each pot. Plant chive seeds in each pot, as directed on the package.

 FACT The plant absorbs light from the sun. Chlorophyll in the leaves traps the light. This is what starts photosynthesis. The plant also absorbs water through its roots and carbon dioxide in the air. Photosynthesis splits the water molecules into hydrogen and oxygen. The oxygen is released into the air. The hydrogen combines with the carbon dioxide to make food for the plant. Without light, photosynthesis can't take place.

3 Cover the holes with soil. Water each pot.

4 Place one pot in a dark room, away from the sun.

TRY THIS Experiment with different sun-loving herbs if you don't like chives. Hardy and tasty herbs, such as thyme and parsley, are good picks. Using edible plants will give you another way to compare your three plants.

5 Place the second pot under a lamp and away from a window.

6 Place the third pot on a windowsill.

7 Let the seeds grow for 2 to 3 weeks, watering when the soil looks dry. Record their growth and color each day. Which pot has the most growth? Which has the least? Once the chives have germinated, taste a small bit each day. Record your observations in your records too.

TRY THIS Mint doesn't need a lot of light to grow, but it also enjoys sun when it can get it. Try this experiment again with mint. See how each plant grows in comparison to the chives.

WATER DISPLAY

Plants need water, nutrients, and oxygen. Sometimes soil might not have enough of one or more of those things. Growing plants hydroponically—in water—solves that problem.

YOU'LL NEED

> 32-quart (30-liter) plastic storage container with lid

> 8 seed starter cubes

> ruler

> box cutter

> water

> carrot seeds

> toothpick or small tweezers

> hydroponic fertilizer

STEPS

1   Remove the storage container's lid. Your starter cubes should have a wider lip around the top. Measure the width of the cube underneath the lip.

2   Ask an adult to cut eight evenly spaced squares in the container's lid. The squares should be the same width as your cubes.

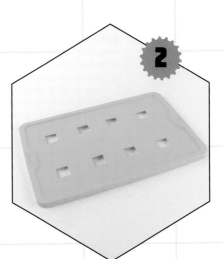

3 Fill the storage container about halfway with water. Soak the cubes for 1 hour.

4 Remove the cubes from the water. Set the lid on the storage container. Press a cube into each of the squares in the lid.

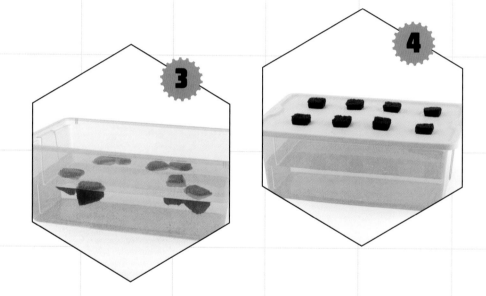

 FACT Seed starter cubes are also called plugs, grow cubes, or rockwool.

5 Carefully place one carrot seed in each cube. Use a toothpick or small tweezers if necessary.

6 Set the storage container in a well-lit area, but out of direct sunlight. Once you've settled on a location, remove one cube. Use the hole to fill the container nearly to the top with water. Replace the cube you removed.

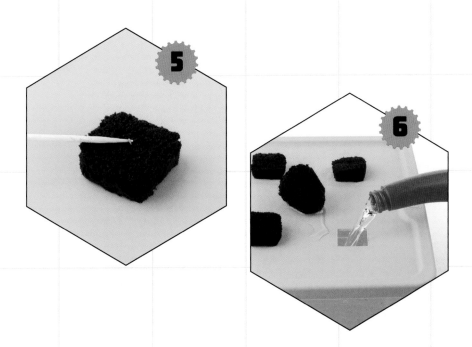

TIP Use an opaque storage container—this means one that you can't see through! If you use a clear bin, algae will grow in the water and steal the oxygen meant for your carrots. Some species of algae release toxins as they die too.

7 Let your seeds grow! With an adult's help, carefully lift the lid. Observe what's happening in the container. When you see roots, add a little hydroponic fertilizer by following the guidelines on the fertilizer package. This is the nutrient solution.

8 Check your carrots every few days. Record how both the tops and the roots are growing, as well as the water level. You should have carrots ready to eat in about two months.

7

TIP Make sure you start with enough water! The roots of your carrots should never dry out. But you also can't add more water, or the roots will drown. When the nutrient solution is gone, you will need to harvest or transplant your crop. You can start over with new seeds or seedlings though.

FACT This method of hydroponic growing is called the Kratky method. The starter cubes provide the seeds with enough nutrients until their roots reach the fertilized water. The plant's upper roots—the carrots—are oxygen-absorbing. They become thicker to absorb more oxygen. The roots in the water—the white parts—are nutrient absorbing. The nutrient solution drops as it's absorbed, but the lower roots continue to grow to reach the solution.

ICE-CREAM PARTY

Studying how a substance changes can be fun. It can also be delicious! Use your chemistry skills to turn liquid into a solid using three different methods. Then compare the results—by tasting them!

MASON JAR ICE-CREAM

You might picture a mad scientist mixing liquids together. But why mix when shaking is so much more fun?

YOU'LL NEED

> 1 cup (240 mL) heavy whipping cream

> 1 ½ tablespoons (23 g) sugar

> ½ teaspoon (2.5 mL) vanilla extract

> pinch salt

> 1 quart (1 liter) mason jar with lid

STEPS

1. Pour all the ingredients into the mason jar. Seal the lid tightly.

2. Shake the jar until the cream thickens, about 5 to 10 minutes. It should double in volume.

FACT What happens when you shake the jar? Air bubbles enter the mixture, whipping it. This is why your ice-cream mixture doubles in volume. Without air, your ice-cream would be too hard to scoop. Fat molecules are broken up. They form walls around the air bubbles, holding the liquid, fat, and air together. This makes your ice-cream smooth. The sugar bonds with the water in the milk and cream. It lowers the freezing point of the ice-cream. The more sugar you add, the softer your ice-cream will be.

TRY THIS To make whipped cream, freeze your jar for 15 minutes before adding the ingredients. Then shake until the mixture is doubled in volume. Eat immediately instead of freezing.

3 Set the jar in a freezer for at least 3 hours, or until solid.

TRY THIS To make butter, leave out the sugar and vanilla. Shake until you hear something solid in your jar—about 10 to 15 minutes. By overshaking, you've forced the fat molecules to break, releasing the air molecules. Then the fat molecules clump together to make butter. The leftover liquid is buttermilk.

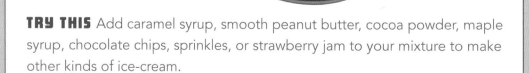

TRY THIS Add caramel syrup, smooth peanut butter, cocoa powder, maple syrup, chocolate chips, sprinkles, or strawberry jam to your mixture to make other kinds of ice-cream.

FREEZER BAG ICE-CREAM

Mason Jar Ice-Cream is delicious, but you might work up a sweat making it! Cool down a little by using salt and ice cubes to speed up the process.

YOU'LL NEED

> ½ cup (120 mL) half and half

> 1 tablespoon (15 g) sugar

> 1 teaspoon (5 mL) vanilla extract

> sandwich-sized zip-top bag

> gallon (3.8 liter) zip-top bag

> crushed ice

> ½ cup (114 g) kosher salt

STEPS

1. Pour the half and half, sugar, and vanilla extract into the small zip-top bag.

2. Close the zipper on the bag. Make sure it's tightly sealed.

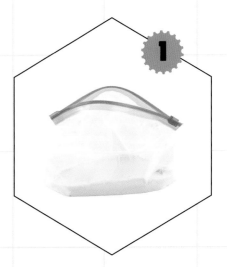

 FACT The fat in cream and half and half is what makes your ice-cream creamy. When fat freezes, it stays in blobs or only crystallizes a little bit. But cream and half and half also contain water, which freeze into crystals. If your ice-cream freezes slowly, like with your Mason Jar Ice-Cream, drops of liquid water will attach themselves to ice crystals. This makes your ice-cream more grainy. By using ice to make and cool the Freezer Bag Ice-Cream, more of the liquid in your mixture freezes. Put your Freezer Bag Ice-Cream in a container and then freeze for 2 to 3 hours. Then compare the two ice-creams again.

3 Put the small bag inside the large bag.

4 Fill the large bag with crushed ice. Add the kosher salt. Close the bag.

5 Shake, smash, twist, and toss the bag around until the half and half mixture thickens into ice-cream.

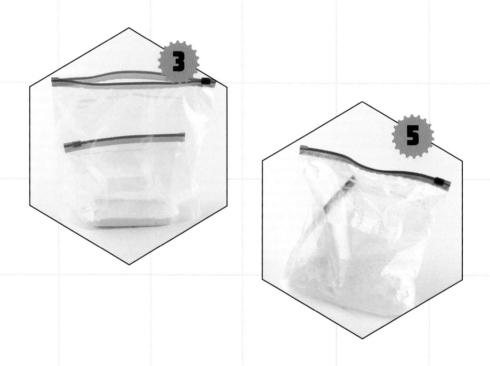

 FACT Adding salt to the ice lowers its freezing point. That means it will freeze at a lower temperature than the normal 32 degrees F (0 degrees Celsius). When the ice in the plastic bag melts, it absorbs energy in the form of heat from the cream mixture. Since the cream mixture's heat is transferred to the ice, the cream gets colder.

6 Remove the small bag from the large bag. Run the small bag briefly under cold water to rinse off any salt, and pat dry. Cut a corner off the bag and squeeze the ice-cream into a dish to eat. You can also eat it right out of the bag!

TRY THIS Compare your Mason Jar and Freezer Bag Ice-Creams. Note any differences in taste, texture, or appearance. What do you think caused those differences?

DELICIOUS DRY ICE-CREAM

You've learned what makes ice-cream grainy. This activity results in a smoother texture. Can you guess why?

YOU'LL NEED

> 2 cups (480 mL) heavy whipping cream

> 2 cups half-and-half

> 1 cup (227 g) sugar

> 2 teaspoons (10 mL) vanilla extract

> stand mixer with paddle attachment

> thick leather or fabric gloves

> ½ pound (225 grams) dry ice

> gallon (3.8 L) zip-top freezer bag

> kitchen towel

> rolling pin

> wooden or plastic spoon

STEPS

1 Measure and pour the whipping cream, half-and-half, sugar, and vanilla into the stand mixer's bowl.

2 Mix for 1 minute to dissolve the sugar.

3 Ask an adult to put on the gloves and then place the dry ice in the gallon zip-top freezer bag. Zip the bag 2/3 closed.

4 Cover the bag with a kitchen towel. Crush the ice with a rolling pin until it is a fine powder.

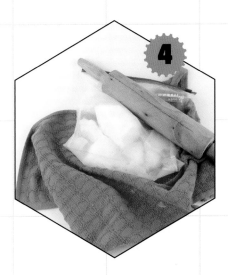

TIP Dry ice is solid carbon dioxide. It has a temperature of -109.3 degrees Fahrenheit (-78.5 degrees Celsius). Always handle dry ice with fabric or leather gloves—never with bare hands!

 FACT When water freezes into ice, the water molecules turn into ice crystals. The lower the temperature, the more quickly the water freezes and the smaller the ice crystals. The warmer the temperature, the slower the water turns to ice. This means the ice crystals are larger. Large ice crystals can affect ice-cream's texture, making it grainy. Dry ice is colder than water ice. And the stand mixer stirs the ice-cream as it freezes, which prevents large ice crystals from forming.

5 Ask an adult to turn on the mixer to medium low. Have them use the spoon to add the dry ice to the bowl very slowly, one small spoonful at a time. If you add it too quickly, the ice-cream will bubble over and make a mess.

6 When the mixture begins to freeze, stop adding the dry ice. Keep mixing for 2 to 3 minutes.

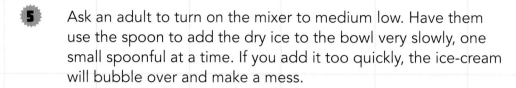

TRY THIS Compare all three of your ice-creams side by side. Note any differences in taste, texture, or appearance. What do you think caused those differences?

You have lots of ice-cream. Now what do you do with it? Celebrate science with a frosty float, and compare your ice-cream's air bubbles while you're at it.

YOU'LL NEED

> tall, clear plastic cups

> straws

> Mason Jar Ice-Cream

> Freezer Bag Ice-Cream

> Delicious Dry Ice-Cream

> root beer

STEPS

1 Set two plastic cups on your work surface. Add a straw to each.

2 Choose one of your ice-creams to use. Place one scoop of ice-cream in the first cup.

FACT Root beer is a carbonated drink. Carbonation is created when carbon dioxide is combined with water at a high pressure. When you open a can or bottle of soda, the gas is released, making your drink fizzy. The air bubbles in the ice-cream help release the carbon dioxide in the soda. At the same time, the soda helps free the ice-cream's air bubbles. The fat in the ice-cream surrounds the released bubbles, creating the fluffy foam at the top of the float.

3   Pour root beer over the ice-cream.

4   Fill the second cup halfway with root beer.

5   Add a scoop of ice-cream.

6   Compare the two cups. Identify the solid, liquid, and gas in each cup. Which float made the best foam?

 FACT When you add the ice-cream to the root beer, fewer bubbles are created. The soda released some of its carbon dioxide into the air while you were scooping the ice-cream. But the remaining carbon dioxide was trapped beneath the ice-cream after you added it to the glass.

When you pour the root beer over the ice-cream, the root beer touches all the ice-cream, not just the bottom. This helps more carbon dioxide bubbles grow, creating more foam.

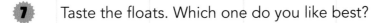 Taste the floats. Which one do you like best?

8 When you've decided which float you like best, make more floats with the other two types of ice-cream. Record the reactions for each. Then taste!

TRY THIS If root beer isn't for you, try cola. Orange or grape soda works too. Swap vanilla ice-cream for chocolate to make a chocolate cow!

READ MORE

Heinecke, Liz Lee. *STEAM Lab for Kids: 52 Creative Hands-On Projects Exploring Science, Technology, Engineering, Art, and Math*. Beverly, Mass.: Quarry Books, 2018.

Latta, Sara L. *Positive Reaction!: A Crash Course in Science*. Savvy. North Mankato, Minn.: Capstone Press, 2015.

Weakland, Mark. *Kaboom!: Wile E. Coyote Experiments with Chemical Reactions*. North Mankato, Minn.: Capstone Press, 2017.

INTERNET SITES

Use FactHound to find Internet sites related to this book.
Visit *www.facthound.com*
Just type in 9781543528480 and go.

 Check out projects, games and lots more at
www.capstonekids.com